Written by Irsa Jawed

Illustrations by Spectacokids

When I Am Frustrated

This Book Belongs To:

To my children, Ashar, Zidan and Ayat.

Copyright © 2021 by Irsa Jawed

ISBN: 9798723568907

No part of this book may be reproduced in any form without permission in writing from the publisher

For more information contact Irsa Jawed at

Spectacokids@gmail.com

Hi, my name is Catty! I am a happy cat most of the time, but sometimes I feel **frustrated** and that is **okay**. Frustration is feeling sad or upset about something. Let's look at what might frustrate me and what I need to do when I am feeling it.

I might feel frustrated when I don't like something.

I might feel frustrated when I make a mistake.

F
A
A

I might feel frustrated when someone yells or says "No!" to me.

When I am frustrated, I can **use** my **words** to talk about my feelings to a friend.

I have a hard
time doing it,
you know?

When I am frustrated, I can take deep breaths to relax my mind and body.

When I am frustrated, I can count till 10.

When I am frustrated, I can go for a walk and get some fresh air.

Instead of yelling, I can use my words and ask for help when I am feeling frustrated.

LIBRARY
Help me,
please?

Instead of yelling, I can use my words and **ask for a break** when I am feeling frustrated.

May I take a break, please?

Instead of yelling, I can use my words and **tell everyone** why I am frustrated.

Oh no, my Ice cream! I am so upset.
ICE CREAM

When I am frustrated, I can ask my mummy or daddy for any kind of help.

When I am frustrated, I need to remember to keep my hands to myself and make good choices.